LAND OF LIBERTY

AMERICA'S NATIONAL PARKS

LYNN M. STONE

Rourke
Publishing LLC
Vero Beach, Florida 32964

www.rourkepublishing.com

PHOTO CREDITS: All photos © Lynn M. Stone except page 9 © Steve Warble

Cover Photo: *Glacier National Park, Montana, is the home of mountain goats, grizzlies, and meadows of wildflowers.*

Editor: Frank Sloan

Cover and page design by Nicola Stratford

Library of Congress Cataloging-in-Publication Data

Stone, Lynn M.
  America's national parks / Lynn M. Stone.
      p. cm. — (Land of liberty)
Summary: Discusses the history and purpose of national parks and describes some prominent examples including Denali National Park in Alaska and Saguaro National Park in Arizona.
Includes bibliographical references and index.
  ISBN 1-58952-313-X (hardcover)
  1. National parks and reserves—United States—Juvenile literature.
[1. National parks and reserves.] I. Title.
  E160 .S76 2002
  973—dc21

                                                                    2002004158

Printed in the USA

MP/W

Table of Contents

Redwoods, the world's tallest trees, stand in the deep, damp forests of Redwood National Park (California).

The National Parks

You are part owner of the tallest trees in the world and the tallest mountain in North America. You are also part owner of several volcanoes, the largest marsh in North America, and huge bat caves. These natural wonders and many more are found in America's national parks. And the national parks are owned by all of us.

Public Land

National parks are huge pieces of **public** land that have been set aside by the United States Government. Each park protects a very special place.

The park road in Denali National Park winds toward Mount McKinley, the highest point in North America (Alaska).

Summer melt from a glacier in Katmai National Park fills a lake (Alaska).

National parks protect natural features, like rivers, mountains, forests, canyons, and **glaciers**. Some protect a historic feature, like Indian cliff dwellings.

George Catlin

George Catlin was a painter of Native Americans, at that time called American Indians. Even in 1832 Catlin feared that the Indians' way of life and the Western wilderness were in danger. He suggested that the government should create "a magnificent park."

An example of one of the "magnificent parks" that George Catlin imagined: Grand Canyon (Arizona).

The canyon and falls of Yellowstone River (Wyoming, Montana)

The First National Park

Catlin's idea did not catch on quickly. But in 1872 **Congress** made the beautiful Yellowstone River country of the Montana and Wyoming **territories** a national park. Yellowstone was the first national park in the world.

Making the Yellowstone country a national park meant that it could not be made into cities, farms, or mines. In addition, hunting would not be allowed. The Yellowstone country would be kept forever as nature had made it.

The National Park Service

By 1916 America had 14 national parks, including Glacier, Mount Rainier, Acadia, and Rocky Mountain. The National Park Service was born. Its job was to manage the parks and certain other public lands.

Rocky Mountain National Park protects alpine wilderness (Colorado).

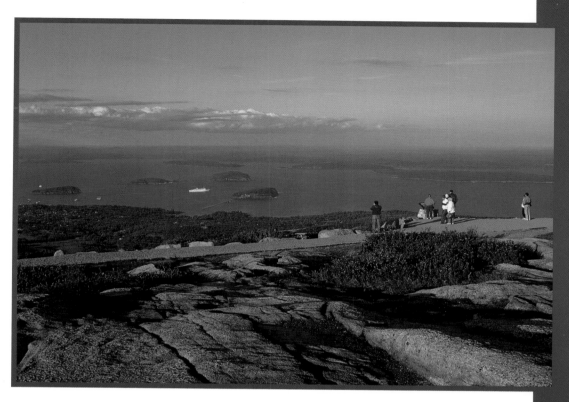

Visitors to Acadia National Park enjoy the early morning view from Cadillac Mountain (Maine).

Today the National Park Service watches over nearly 60 national parks and 350 other public places. These can be found across the nation.

The idea of national parks has become one of America's gifts to the world. Dozens of other countries have created their own national parks.

Enjoying Our National Parks

Most of America's national parks have some paved roads, restaurants, and hotels. But the national parks also have thousands of square miles of wilderness. Quiet footpaths lead to mountain peaks, canyon floors, **tide pools**, wildflower gardens, and thundering waterfalls.

A footpath snakes its way through alpine meadows toward Mount Rainier in Mount Rainier National Park (Washington).

Katmai National Park is home to some 2,000 grizzly bears (Alaska).

Visiting National Parks

Each national park is a treasure. Let's visit a few. Denali National Park in Alaska has snow-covered Mount McKinley. At 20,320 feet (6,194 meters), McKinley is North America's tallest mountain. Alaska's Katmai National Park is famous for its volcanoes and brown bears.

Glacier National Park in Montana is the mountain home of grizzly bears and mountain goats.

Redwood National Park in California has the world's tallest trees. Farther south in California, Yosemite has the world's largest living things—Sequoia trees.

A rainbow arches across Swiftcurrent Lake in Glacier National Park (Montana).

Everglades National Park protects the plants and animals of America's greatest wetland (Florida).

Florida's Everglades National Park has much wildlife. This includes America's largest freshwater marsh, alligators, and many long-legged wading birds.

Yellowstone is one of the greatest natural areas on earth. It has glaciers and **geysers**, hot springs, snowy peaks, and an amazing variety of wildlife. Grizzlies, wolves, elk, white pelicans, and trumpeter swans are among the creatures that live there.

Saguaro National Park in Arizona is the desert home of huge saguaro cactuses.

Saguaro National Park is home to the mighty saguaro cactus and Sonoran Desert wildlife (Arizona).

The largest national park is Wrangell-St. Elias in Alaska. Together with the Wrangell-St. Elias Preserve, it is larger than Vermont and New Hampshire combined! Great Smoky Mountain National Park in North Carolina and Tennessee has the most visitors each year.

The national parks protect nature's wonders for all of us forever.

National parks are places for people as well as wildlife (Theodore R. Roosevelt National Park, North Dakota).

Glossary

Congress (KAHN gress) – the elected body of United States senators and representatives who meet in Washington, D.C.

geyser (GUY zuhr) – a spring that sometimes shoots steam and hot water into the air

glacier (GLAY shur) – a large river of ice that moves very slowly down a slope or valley

public (PUB lik) – the people as an entire group

territories (TERR uh TOR eez) – land masses owned by the United States that are not part of the 50 states

tide pool (TIED POOL) – the rocky seashore basins that remain filled with seawater each time the ocean tide retreats

Index

Further Reading

Fazio, Wende. *Everglades National Park.* Children's Press, 1998

Petersen, David. *National Parks.* Children's Press, 2001

Websites to Visit

National Parks Foundation at
      http://www.nationalparks.org/index.html

National Park Service at http://www.nps.gov/parks.html

U.S. National Parks at http://www.us-national-parks.net

About the Author

Lynn Stone is the author of over 400 children's nonfiction books. He is a talented natural history photographer as well. Lynn, a former teacher, travels worldwide to photograph wildlife in its natural habitat.